Jean-Pierre Filiu & David B.

BEST OF ENEMIES

A History of US and Middle East Relations

Part One: 1783-1953

First published in English in 2012
by SelfMadeHero
5 Upper Wimpole Street
London WIG 6BP
www.selfmadehero.com

Written by: Jean-Pierre Filiu and David B.
Illustrated by: David B.
Translated from the French edition by Edward Gauvin

**INSTITUT
FRANÇAIS**

This book is supported by the Institut français
as part of the Burgess programme
(www.frenchbooknews.com)

Editorial and Lettering: Lizzie Kaye
Marketing Director: Doug Wallace
Publishing Director: Emma Hayley
With thanks to: Nick de Somogyi
David B. font provided by Coconino Press

First published in French by Futuropolis in 2011
© Futuropolis, Paris, 2011

A CIP record for this book is available from the British Library

ISBN: 978-1-906838-45-4

10 9 8 7 6 5 4 3 2 1

Printed and bound in China

Jean-Pierre Filiu & David B.

BEST OF ENEMIES

A History of US and Middle East Relations

Part One: 1783-1953

1 An Old Story

This is the story of two men who lived 4,600 years ago.

If we want a roof for the temple, we must first raise columns.

Gilgamesh was the king of the city of Uruk, and Enkidu was his friend.

For that, we need such giant trees as do not grow nearby.

They grow in the Cedar Forest.

The Cedar Forest?

But it is guarded by the demon Humbaba!

His weapons are fearsome, and he possesses the Seven Splendors!

Once more, we stand alone between a world of peace and a world of fear and chaos.

Once more, we are called upon to defend the safety of our people and the hopes of all humanity. We accept this responsibility.

Humbaba can only use the Seven Splendors to threaten, frighten, and destroy.

To bring upon us such a day of horror as we have never seen.

We shall do everything in our power to ensure that day never comes.

2

If Humbaba is not Evil, then Evil has no meaning!

We alone stand between freedom and fear, our people's safety and an evil with which there can be no reconciliation, whose victory cannot be permitted. Humanity depends on our success.

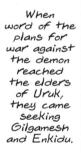

When word of the plans for war against the demon reached the elders of Uruk, they came seeking Gilgamesh and Enkidu.

You are young, Gilgamesh, and your heart rash. Beware the consequences of your actions.

It is just as dangerous to take action as it is to do nothing. There are things we know, and we know we know them. These are Known Knowns. There are also things we know we don't know. These are Known unKnowns.

But there are also unknown unknowns — the ones we don't know we don't know. What does this tell us? That the world we live in is vast and difficult, a complicated world where denial and manipulation are common currency.

We do not claim to know all the ways of Providence...

...yet we can trust in them, placing our confidence in the loving God behind all of life and all of history.

Gilgamesh and Enkidu had the city's blacksmiths forge them terrible weapons of great mass.

They set out for the Cedar Forest.

4

They entered the woods in search of the demon.

At the heart of the Forest, gods appeared to warn them of the consequences of their actions. They asked that Humbaba be spared.

We ask no reward but a lasting peace. And accept no result but a total and definitive success.

War is not a walk in the park. War is hard, people get killed. It's dangerous.

After the encounter with the gods, Humbaba burst forth from between the trees.

The Seven Splendors did not protect the demon from defeat.

Contrary to the wishes of the gods, Enkidu killed Humbaba.

The demon's body disappeared beneath the trunks of cedars that Gilgamesh and his friend felled.

They would be able to finish their temple.

But when they returned to Uruk, Enkidu died. For disobeying them, the gods caused his death.

Gilgamesh they spared, for there must be one left behind to suffer.

He realized the consequences of death and destruction.

The king of Uruk crossed the mountain, which was an image of the Far-Away, in search of Utnapishtim the immortal, in order to Know the secret of life and death.

He drew close enough to this secret to touch it, but it slipped his grasp. He returned to his city, wise from the hardships he had endured in his journey.

To this day, the Epic of Gilgamesh remains among the most ancient texts yet discovered. It left its mark on every civilization in the region. Versions of it exist in Sumerian, Babylonian, Hittite, and Assyrian; there are even traces of it in the Bible.

This story was being told in Iraq some four thousand years ago.

The U.S. invasion of Iraq in 2003 plunged the country into the strife of civil war and occupation.

We have mischievously placed words spoken by George W. Bush and Donald Rumsfeld from 2002 and 2003 into the mouths of Gilgamesh and Enkidu.

In times of tragedy, faith assures us that death and suffering are not the final word, that love and hope are eternal.

During a war the kind of "evidence" people are looking for usually doesn't exist.

As though warnings of the disasters of war— uttered millennia ago in the very region where tragedy today unfolds— had gone unheard.

Acts of cruelty speak to one another across time.

In the Louvre is a Sumerian stele discovered in Iraq.

It depicts the battle of the Prince of Lagash against the city of Umma.

Archeologists have named it the Stele of the Vultures.

On one of its fragments, the bodies of the vanquished lie piled in a monument to victory.

In 2004, in the prison at Abu Ghraib, American soldiers — at once unfamiliar with the Epic of Gilgamesh and the Stele of the Vultures...

...and yet distant heirs, through the Bible and Christianity, to this past—

forced their prisoners to pile on top of one another, and had photos taken with them.

The photos of those tortured at Abu Ghraib are a Stele of the Vultures for our century.

2 Piracy

For centuries, Christian and Muslim pirates traded blow for blow in the Mediterranean.

At the end of the 15th century, the Muslims, making the most of Ottoman conquests, gained the upper hand.

The capital of the maritime jihad was Algiers, which the Barbarossa brothers held for the Sultan in Constantinople.

In 1571, a colossal battle broke out in the Gulf of Lepanto between a Christian coalition and the Turks.

The Muslim armada met with a crushing defeat.

It would prove the end of Ottoman attempts to conquer the Mediterranean Basin.

But from the ports of Morocco, Algiers, Tunis, and Tripoli, the raids continued.

In vain did the English, French, Spanish, and Dutch fleets go to bombard Algiers and Tunis during the 17th and 18th centuries.

Christian ships were boarded, their crews and passengers enslaved.

The slaves met with various fates. Women became servants or were placed in harems.

Children were forcibly converted and educated to become soldiers, sailors, or civil servants in the Turkish administration.

Men who consented to convert to Islam became pirates in turn.

According to the accounts of witnesses, such defectors proved the worst enemies of their former fellow believers, and the cruelest tormentors of slaves who had remained Christian.

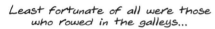

Least fortunate of all were those who rowed in the galleys...

...until, with the rise of sailing ships, there was no more use for galley slaves.

The cities then sent them to labor on public buildings or at sites outside the battlements.

They were starved and beaten, and every hardship was visited upon them for continuing to practice their religion.

The luckiest were bought by private individuals and became household servants.

They could, according to their abilities, rise to the more prestigious posts of steward or personal secretary.

In general, treatment differed from reign to reign. Severe in Morocco, it was gentler in Tunisia, where slaves were afforded certain advantages.

At the beginning of the 19th century, the three naval powers of France, England, and Spain could buy peace in exchange for tribute.

Lesser powers like Denmark, Holland, and the Italian states had no choice but to be targets of commercial raiding, and to ransom their captured crews.

To the Algerians, the English hinted that since America had become an independent state, its ships were no longer protected by the British fleet.

It was what the English called fair play.

In 1785, the Algerians captured several American trading vessels, one after the other.

Thus did the public learn of the Barbary pirates.

THE MONITOR

At the time, the young nation was still a vast but sparsely populated land—around three million inhabitants, counting slaves—nor was it an economic power.

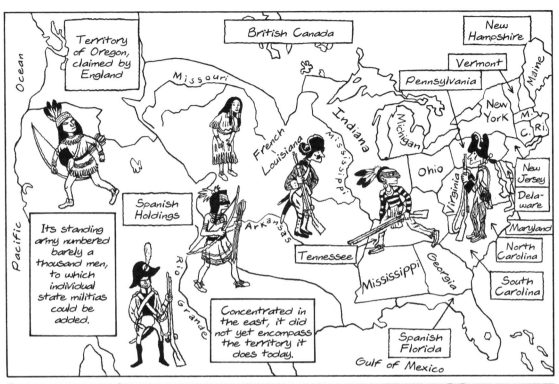

Ocean

Pacific

Territory of Oregon, claimed by England

British Canada

Missouri

French Louisiana

Indiana

Mississippi

Michigan

Ohio

New Hampshire

Vermont

Pennsylvania

New York

Maine

M.

C. R.i

Spanish Holdings

Arkansas

Tennessee

Virginia

New Jersey

Dela-ware

Maryland

North Carolina

South Carolina

Its standing army numbered barely a thousand men, to which individual state militias could be added.

Rio Grande

Concentrated in the east, it did not yet encompass the territory it does today.

Spanish Florida

Georgia

Mississippi

Gulf of Mexico

Apart from the Indians, the Americans were not at war with anyone.

And so America was no sooner born than it found itself at war with countries thousands of miles away.

Congress allotted $80,000 to buy peace with the Barbary Coast.

The Algerians demanded much more money, and negotiations were difficult. It took ten years to reach the agreement that saw enslaved sailors freed.

Morocco was the first to sign, for $20,000.

In 1786, the U.S. attempted to conclude a treaty with the regency of Tripoli.

Russian Empire

Sweden

Poland

Ireland

England

Atlantic Ocean

Kingdom of France

Austrian Empire

Ottorman Empire

Portugal

Kingdom of Spain

Rabat

Algiers

Algeria

Tunis

Tripoli

Mediterranean Sea

Tri poli

Egypt

Morocco

Tunisia

The meeting between the American and Tripolitan plenipotentiaries took place in London.

John Adams, U.S. Ambassador in London.

The translator. His name is unknown. Doubtless a defector who spoke English or French.

Thomas Jefferson, U.S. Ambassador in Paris.

Sidi Haji Abdrahaman, Tripolitan envoy.

20

The ambassador's offered $20,000 to the Regency's representative, who found it too modest a sum.

The thing was, the Algerians were about to get much more.

These waters belong to us!

It is the right and duty of all Muslims to wage jihad against the infidel.

Servitude is the infidel's natural lot.

The negotiations dragged along.

This was also due to the conflicting attitudes of the two American ambassadors.

For just as Adams was conciliatory...

...so Jefferson was sarcastic and aggressive.

SLAVERY!

2500 dollars

When the Libyan representative pointed out that the U.S. was also a slave-owning country, Jefferson grew outraged.

There could be no comparison between slavery in the Barbary Coast and his own practices, as he claimed to treat his slaves "humanely".

Negotiations failed.

In 1796, the Tripolitan pirates captured two American vessels and enslaved their crews. With this leverage, they obtained a peace treaty with favorable terms.

In 1797, Adams became the second president of the United States. His administration settled with the Barbary States for a fifth of the country's budget.

In 1801, it was Jefferson's turn to be president, and to confront the problem of piracy and the tributes it demanded.

These sums are money thrown to the winds!

The demands of different sultans, beys, and pashas increased unceasingly, each insisting on as much or more than his neighbor. As the Pasha of Tripoli said to Consul James Cathcart:

It is true that you have paid me for the peace; but you have given me nothing to maintain it.

So saying, the Pasha Yusuf Karamanli expelled the consul and declared war on the U.S.

He knew little of the land he was preparing to fight.

In the complex Orient of the time, most people barely knew the American continent existed.

But centuries of holy war on the seas confirmed Yusuf Karamanli in his decision.

And yet his dynasty was recent, less than a century old. His ancestor Ahmad had received his power from the hands of the Ottoman sultan in 1711.

Under his family, the city of Tripoli had prospered, thanks to the trade and efficacy of its pirates.

24

Beginning in 1782, a plague, then a famine, ravaged Tripoli, resulting in the Regency's decline.

These hardships led to civil war, and only in 1791 could Yusuf Karamanli take back the reins of power from the Algerian adventurer who had seized them.

But even if his power depended, in principle, on the Sultan of Constantinople, he made his own policies...

...not hesitating to parley with Napoleon Bonaparte, who at the time was running rampant over Egypt, a province of the Ottoman Empire.

Beyond the Mediterranean, across the Atlantic, President Jefferson decided to send a squadron against the Pasha of Tripoli.

Members of Congress who had not been consulted were furious. The expedition would cost twice as much as the Barbary tribute.

Four ships crossed the ocean to blockade the port of Tripoli.

But as their drafts were too great to navigate the reefs and shallows of the port, they were forced to keep their distance.

It was easy for Tripolitan feluccas to slip along the coast and escape their watch.

Soon the American flotilla faced the problem of securing fresh water.

Lieutenant Sterret, in charge of the Enterprise, was dispatched to Malta to get drinking water for the whole squadron.

Ship to port, sir!

The ship crossed the path of a Regency ship: the Tripoli.

They're hoisting their flag.

It was a ship of 14 cannon, with a crew of 80 men.

Lieutenant Sterret employed a ruse of war and hoisted British colors.

Prepare to fire.

I am Mohammad Rous. My country is at war with the Americans. I must attack their ships.

27

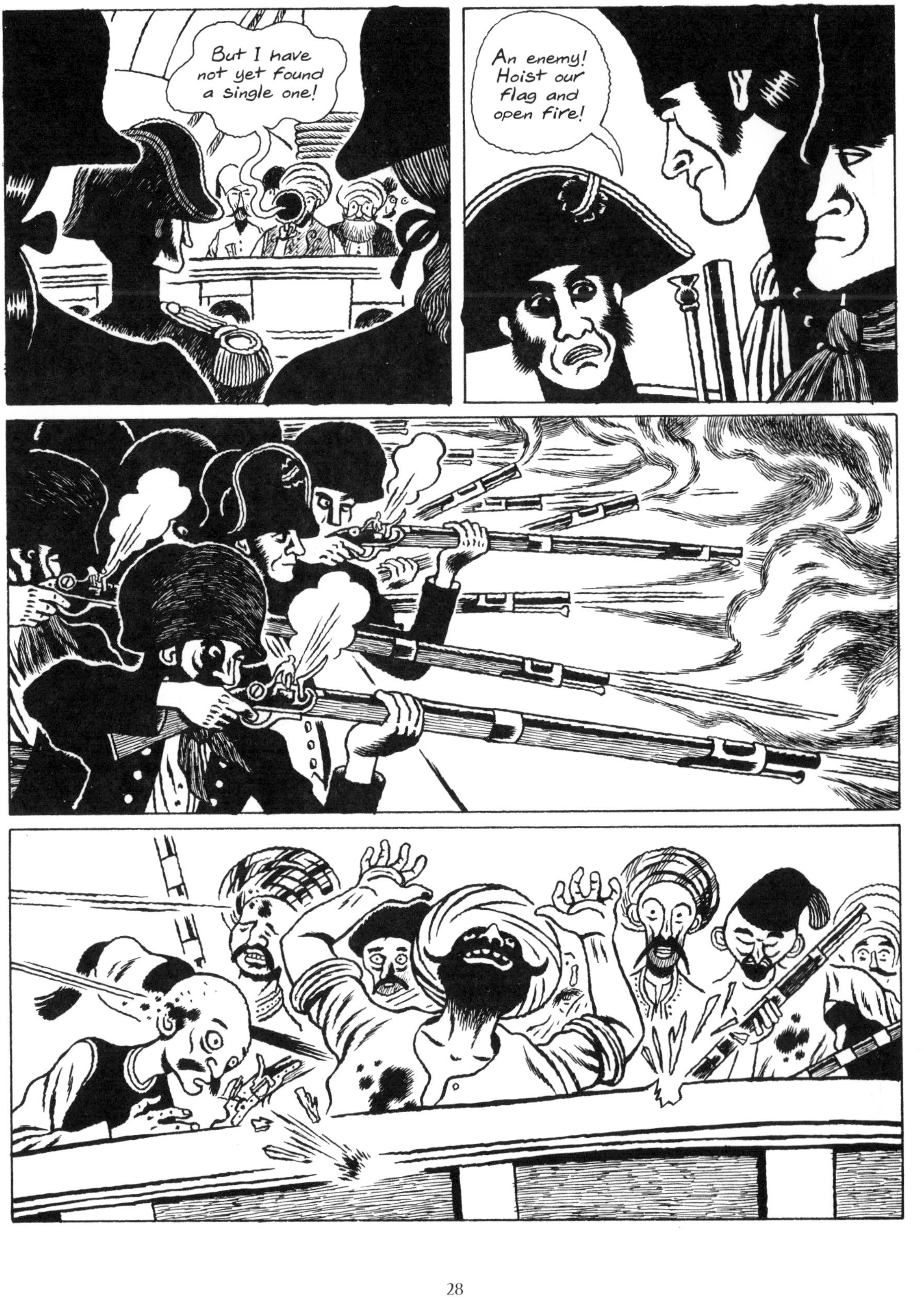
But I have not yet found a single one!
An enemy! Hoist our flag and open fire!

AMERICANS! CANNONS, EVERYONE! OPEN FIRE!

The Tripoli tried to ram the Enterprise, which evaded them. The Barbary pirates then tried to board.

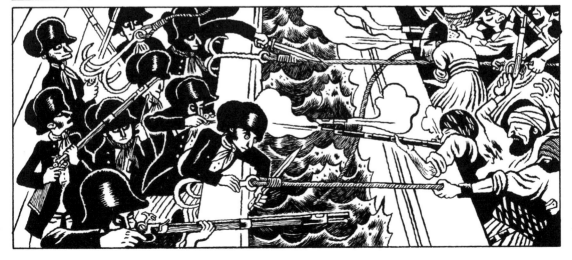

The attempt was repulsed.

Lower the flag!

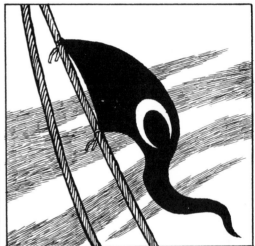

They're lowering the flag! They surrender! We must cease fire.

Stay on your guard...

They've stopped shooting! Attack! Now!

That trick needs a little more time to work.

But he attacked too early!

The battle went on for three hours.

The Tripolitans alternated several attempts to board...

...with the trick of lowering their flag again, to mimic surrender.

All these attempts failed.

Finish them off. Fire a broadside!

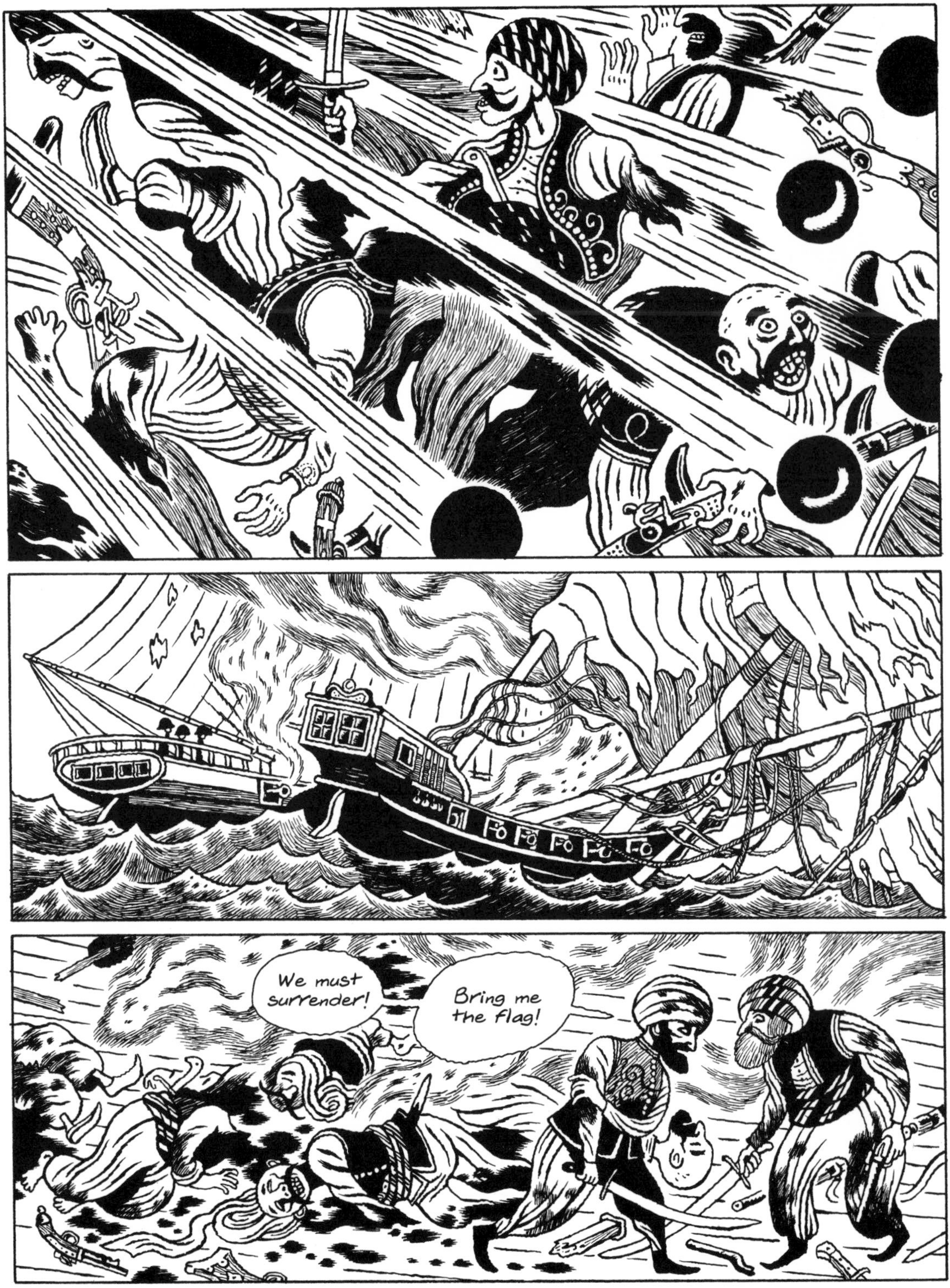
We must surrender!
Bring me the flag!

He threw his flag into the sea!

It can't be a trick now. He surrenders.

Prepare to board!

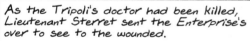

There were 30 dead and 30 wounded aboard the Tripoli.

As the Tripoli's doctor had been killed, Lieutenant Sterret sent the *Enterprise's* over to see to the wounded.

Throw all their weapons overboard!

33

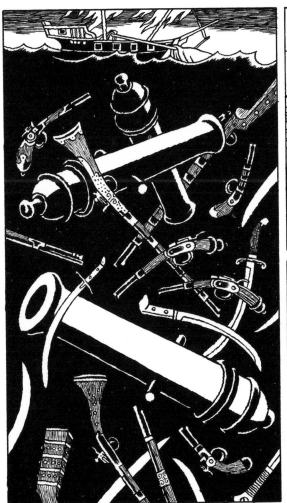

As he had orders against capturing a ship, Lt. Sterret left the Tripoli to its fate.

Captain Mohammad Rous managed to bring his ship back to port.

The Pasha immediately had him demoted and beaten.

The blockade of the port of Tripoli continued, ineffectual as ever. But Lt. Sterret's victory galvanized American public opinion.

President Jefferson obtained the material and legislative means from Congress to fight the pirates

...seize all vessels and goods of the Pasha of Tripoli or his subjects and bring them to port, that they may be disposed of in accordance with the law.

In 1802, a Tripolitan pirate captured the Franklin and enslaved its crew.

A new ransom had to be paid.

Faced with the futility of the blockade, Commodore Dale returned to the U.S. but demanded the rank of admiral.

As the rank did not yet exist in the American Navy, Congress refused to instate it for him.

Furious, Dale left the Navy.

The second expedition, which left in April 1803 under the command of Commodore Morris, obtained results just as meager as the first.

A shipment of flour was blocked along the Tripolitan coast.

To destroy it, the Americans would have to land troops.

Some of the cargo was put to the torch, but only some.

It was the first time in history they had confronted Muslims on solid ground.

That June, a ship in the Pasha's fleet was entirely destroyed.

Thinking he would do no better, Commodore Morris returned home, where he faced a congressional inquiry.

...it is not in the public interest that you any longer retain a command in the U.S. Navy!

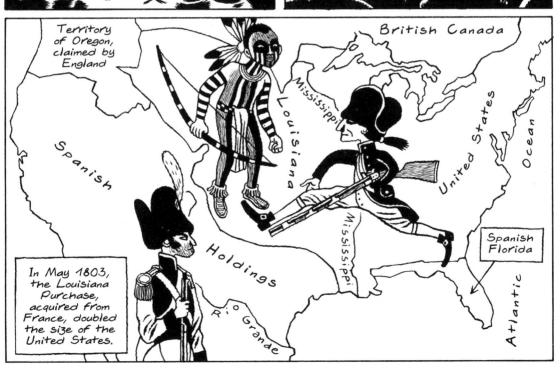

Territory of Oregon, claimed by England

British Canada

Spanish Holdings

Louisiana

Mississippi

Mississippi

United States

Atlantic Ocean

Spanish Florida

Rio Grande

Atlantic

In May 1803, the Louisiana Purchase, acquired from France, doubled the size of the United States.

In Tripoli, Pasha Karamanli called the other Regencies to holy war against the U.S.

Guns, munitions, and supplies arrived from Algiers and Morocco.

Congress decided to send a third expedition, but this time the officer in command had to measure up.

Captain Edward Preble— "an iron fist in an iron glove" sort of officer—was chosen.

On 7 October 1803, the blockade of the port of Tripoli recommenced.

On 31 October, while pursuing a Tripolitan vessel, the *Philadelphia* ran aground in the shallows.

It was immediately surrounded by a flotilla of Regency gunboats, who opened fire.

Fire it could not return, due to its tilt from running aground.

Captain Bainbridge and his crew were forced to surrender.

They were imprisoned in Tripoli. The Pasha immediately demanded a ransom.

At high tide, the Tripolitans raised the Philadelphia and brought it to port.

They even salvaged the cannons the Americans had thrown overboard.

The Pasha was exultant. He had the boat and its crew.

This was no merchant vessel, but a frigate of war.

Moreover, documents had been seized, documents Captain Bainbridge hadn't had time to burn.

They offered precious information on the enemy fleet's plans and potential.

For his part, Commodore Preble was resolved to destroy the *Philadelphia* in the port of Tripoli itself.

On 16 February 1804, two American ships, the *Siren* and the *Intrepid*, approached the harbor.

The *Intrepid* was a Tripolitan vessel, captured earlier and intended to fool the enemy.

With the help of an interpreter who pretended to be the captain, the *Intrepid* entered the harbor and moored near the *Philadelphia*.

Lt. Decatur's men mounted an assault, surprising the Tripolitan crew.

There was no fight. The Tripolitans leapt overboard.

The sailors had only to place explosive charges, light the fuses, and evacuate the *Philadelphia* as quickly as possible.

The explosion occurred just beneath the windows of the Pasha's palace.

Furious at the loss of a negotiation tool, the Pasha had the Philadelphia's men in jail beaten.

Yusuf Karamanli pulled out all the stops. He threatened, negotiated, proposed peace, demanded more money.

Edward Preble fully intended to press home his advantage.

From the King of Naples, he rented gunboats with mortars whose angle would allow them to reach the city's defenses.

Their diminutive size allowed them to enter the harbor and attack the ships there.

Have no fear! Americans are a kind of Jew, and know not how to fight.

The mortars bombarded the city and its walls.

American sailors boarded and captured several ships.

On 30 September 1804, the Danish Consul in Tripoli wrote to Commodore Preble.

"I must tell you that all your fleet's attacks, excepting that of August 3rd, have had little effect and any damage caused was inconsequential."

In fact, the bombardment destroyed the Jewish quarter. Which made the Pasha laugh.

The city held.

An attempt to blow up one of the bastions defending the port with a ship made into a floating bomb ended in failure.

The crew died when the boat exploded prematurely.

Despite all his efforts, Edward Preble was making no headway before Tripoli.

He had to relinquish command to Commodore Barron, who has just arrived from the U.S. with the fourth fleet sent to oppose Tripoli.

With James Barron was William Eaton, who had been consul in Tunis and had an asset in the war against the Regency: Hamet Karamanli, the Pasha's brother.

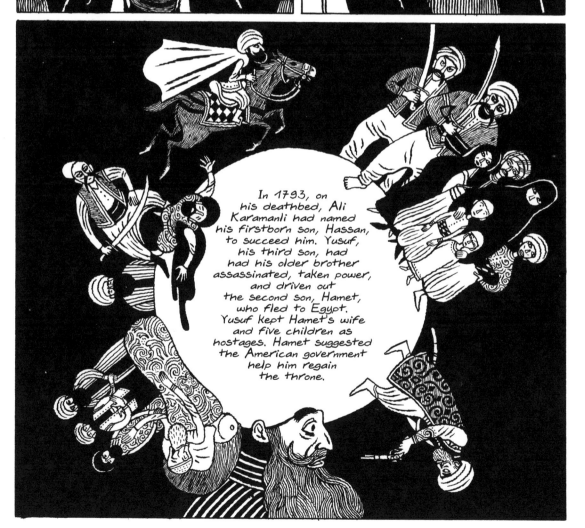

In 1793, on his deathbed, Ali Karamanli had named his firstborn son, Hassan, to succeed him. Yusuf, his third son, had had his older brother assassinated, taken power, and driven out the second son, Hamet, who fled to Egypt. Yusuf kept Hamet's wife and five children as hostages. Hamet suggested the American government help him regain the throne.

Eaton, who was an interventionist, leapt at Hamet's proposition, which promised a very favorable peace.

President Jefferson approved the plan. For the first time in its history, the U.S. would attempt to overthrow the government of a hostile nation.

While Commodore Barron kept up the blockade without bombardment, Consul Tobias Lear undertook new talks with Pasha Yusuf Karamanli, while William Eaton crossed the desert to rejoin Hamet and his supporters.

American politics were playing themselves out on three fronts.

Together, Eaton and Hamet recruited a group of mercenaries: Bedouins, Greek deserters from the Egyptian Army, and adventurers from the Eastern Mediterranean.

Eight American sailors, too, joined the pretender's camp. Five hundred men in all, to conquer Tripoli.

The expedition's first objective was the port of Derna, to the east of Tripoli.

The desert march was torture for everyone.

Fights broke out between Muslims and "infidels" in the ranks, the former threatening to leave or to slaughter the latter.

More money!

Money is the Arabs' god!

It was between Eaton and Hamet Karamanli that the falling-out took place.

We must push on to Derna now!

The men are exhausted. Let us camp here and wait for word!

Refuse to march and you'll have neither food nor water!

Eaton had his men guard the supply tent.

The night passed, everyone watchful and on edge.

In the morning, the Arab riders marched on the tent.

51

They made threats, as if to charge, fell back, and charged again.

The Greeks and the Americans didn't flinch.

After an hour of this stampeding, Hamet's troops lowered their weapons and agreed to go on.

Several days later, they were resupplied by American ships who would support their attack on Derna.

An attack that began with the Argus, the Hornet, and the Nautilus bombarding its fortifications on 26 April 1805.

The defenders fell back toward the city, where they were attacked by men under Hamet Karamanli and William Eaton.

The riders attacked the city from the south.

Arab, Greek, and American infantry mounted an assault on the battlements and barricades.

Lt. O'Bannon planted his flag on the city walls.

Hamet and his allies now had a base for attacking Tripoli. The Pasha's reinforcements arrived too late.

At the news of Derna's fall, the Pasha agreed to Consul Tobias Lear's offer of peace.

Derna was evacuated and returned to Yusuf Karamanli.

To defend himself from an attack by his brother, he obtained a secret clause allowing him to keep one member of Hamet's family hostage.

Both camps saw themselves as winners: the U.S. had obtained its peace, and the prisoners were returned.

But Eaton and the hardliners denounced both the peace Tobias Lear had negotiated and Hamet's abandonment.

Eaton thought the Pasha, in his greatly weakened state, could be toppled and that taking Tripoli would be a lesson to the regencies of Tunis and Algiers.

We do not make peace with a pirate!

But for his government, peace spared lives and American money.

The Pasha could rejoice; he had managed to save face and show the Barbary States one could stand up to the U.S.

For the Algerian pirates, the Americans had proved their weakness by agreeing to peace, and they began to hunt down their ships.

Over the following years, several vessels were attacked or captured.

The War of
1812 arrived
to distract
the Americans'
attention.

The American war
on Algiers resumed
in 1815, with the
capture of several
Barbary ships.

The
arrival of
the American
fleet at the
gates of
Algiers forced
the Bey
to parley.
Prisoners
were freed
and a treaty
signed with
concessions
never before
given to a
Western
power.

In 1816, the English and the Dutch in turn forced treaties just as favorable with the mouths of their cannons.

In 1830, a French expedition seized Algiers, putting an end to the Regency.

It was the end of Barbary piracy in the Mediterranean.

In 1805, the Lewis and Clark expedition reached America's Pacific coast.

In the decades to come, the U.S., by treaty or by conquest, would acquire new territories to the south and west.

Thus did they create a position of centrality for themselves among Asia, Oceania, Europe, and Africa.

3 Oil

Despite signing treaties with the Barbary States, the United States did not establish formal relations with the Ottoman Empire until 1862.

But their representatives in Istanbul were very active in corrupting local officials. In this way, they obtained extraterritorial privileges for U.S. nationals.

At the beginning of the 19th century, it was all the rage to send over missionaries by the hundreds.

Between 1826 and 1841, a third of them fell ill and died shortly after arriving, as sanitary conditions were appalling.

The missionary movement was borne by the same messianic vision that had inspired the taming of the West.

It is our manifest destiny to overspread and to possess the whole of the continent which Providence has given us.

John O'Sullivan.

In 1844, the Reverend George Bush, Professor of Hebrew at New York University and distant ancestor of the two presidents, advocated "restoring the land of Israel to the Jews".

Mohammad is a false prophet!

On his voyage to the Middle East, Mark Twain was highly critical of local religions.

Seeing the true sons of the desert stripped him of romanticism.

The missionaries' Palestine exists only in dreams.

In 1895, the American missionary network in the Middle East consisted of 400 schools, 9 colleges, 9 hospitals, and 10 dispensaries.

But it had only managed to convert a tiny number of locals — usually Eastern Christians, and not Muslims.

In 1902, American officer Alfred Mahan, a theorist of the projection of power, coined the term "Middle East"...

...in order to assert that whoever controlled the "Middle East" would control the world.

However, the U.S. remained neutral from 1914 to 1917...

...and did not intervene in the Anglo-French offensive against the Ottoman Empire.

The activist minorities and their network in the U.S. rejoiced at the collapse of the "Sublime Porte".

Even today, the Middle East is defined by the consequences of Great Britain's three contradictory promises during the hostilities.

The "Arab Kingdom" for Bedouin rebels manipulated by Colonel Lawrence.

The Sykes-Picot Agreement, which would divide colonies with France.

The Balfour declaration in favor of the Zionists.

President Woodrow Wilson stood diametrically opposed to this horse-trading.

He championed the right of a people to self-determination.

Wilson was thwarted by Congress, and the U.S. did not sit in on the League of Nations, founded on his principles.

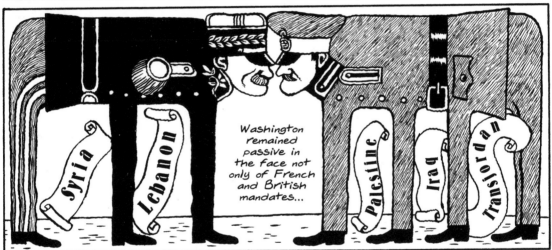

Washington remained passive in the face not only of French and British mandates...

Syria

Lebanon

Palestine

Iraq

Transjordan

...but of nationalist uprisings that flared up in the region.

It was World War II, with its vital need for oil, that drove the U.S. to get involved in the Middle East.

His speech, translated into Arabic, was widely broadcast.

In November 1942, President Roosevelt called the U.S. landing in North Africa "the great jihad of Freedom".

The only country not already under British control that could satisfy the needs of the American military machine was Saudi Arabia.

Its king, Abdul-Aziz Ibn Saud, was 69 years old.

His dynasty could be traced back to the 18th century.

It was born of the meeting between an imam noted for his intolerance, and a tribal chieftain from the Nejd.

The imam Mohammad Ibn Abd-al-Wahhab was driven from Mecca for denouncing the widespread corruption there.

Mohammad ibn Saud ruled the Al-Diriyah oasis where his clan was based.

The imam brought a doctrine to these plundering Bedouins, and their raids became holy wars.

Ibn Abd-al-Wahhab rejected any alteration to Islam, and spat on heretics — that is, anyone who believed differently, but especially Shiites.

66

Soon the Wahhabis set out from Central Arabia to conquer Riyadh, then the region of Al-Ahsa.

In 1802, they captured the Shiite city of Karbala in Iraq and slaughtered the populace.

Its Ottoman governors, equally hostile to Shiites and Wahhabis, had left it unprotected.

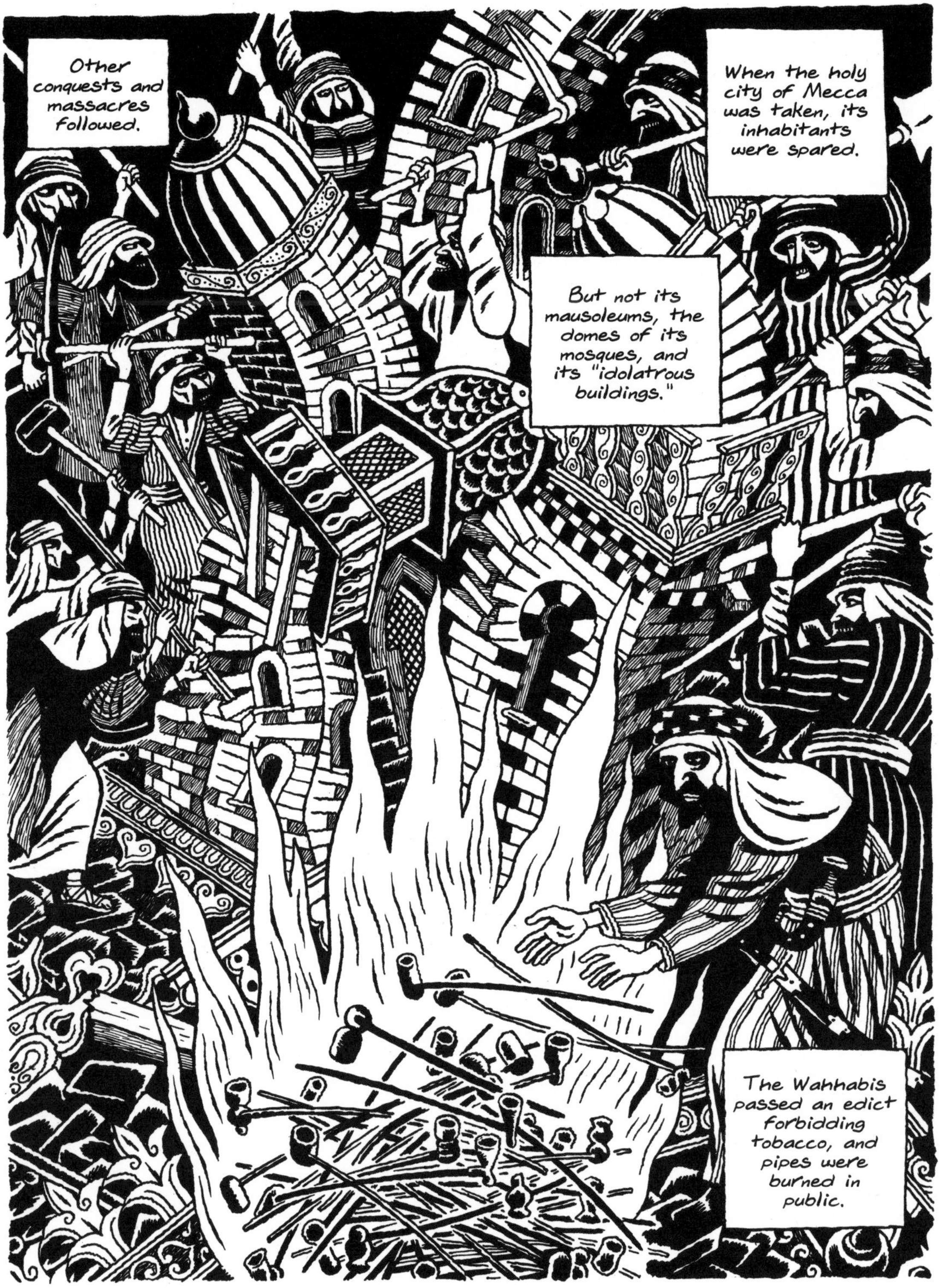
Other conquests and massacres followed.
When the holy city of Mecca was taken, its inhabitants were spared.
But not its mausoleums, the domes of its mosques, and its "idolatrous buildings."
The Wahhabis passed an edict forbidding tobacco, and pipes were burned in public.

These conquests did not go unopposed, and in 1803 the Emir of the Wahhabis was assassinated by a dervish or a Shiite — sources differ.

In 1818, the Ottomans invaded Arabia and took Al-Diriyah after a bloody siege.

The situation stabilized over the course of the 19th century.

A British diplomat said:

Emir Faisal's rule is strict but just.

Where his predecessors failed, he has succeeded in curbing the predatory instincts of the tribes.

While none love the Emir, all admire him, and speak of him with a curious fear, a blend of hatred and respect.

But at the century's end, the Emirate sank into civil war.

The House of Rashid drove the House of Saud from Riyadh in 1891.

In 1889, Abdul-Aziz Ibn Saud's father held a banquet for members of the House of Rashid. The thirteen-year old Abdul-Aziz watched as they were slaughtered on his father's orders.

At the age of 25, after taking back Riyadh, he became the chief of the Wahhabites.

He led a war against the Hashemite rulers of Mecca, which he seized in 1924.

The revolt of the Ikhwan, his former supporters, was put down by the British, who decimated them with bombs and machine guns.

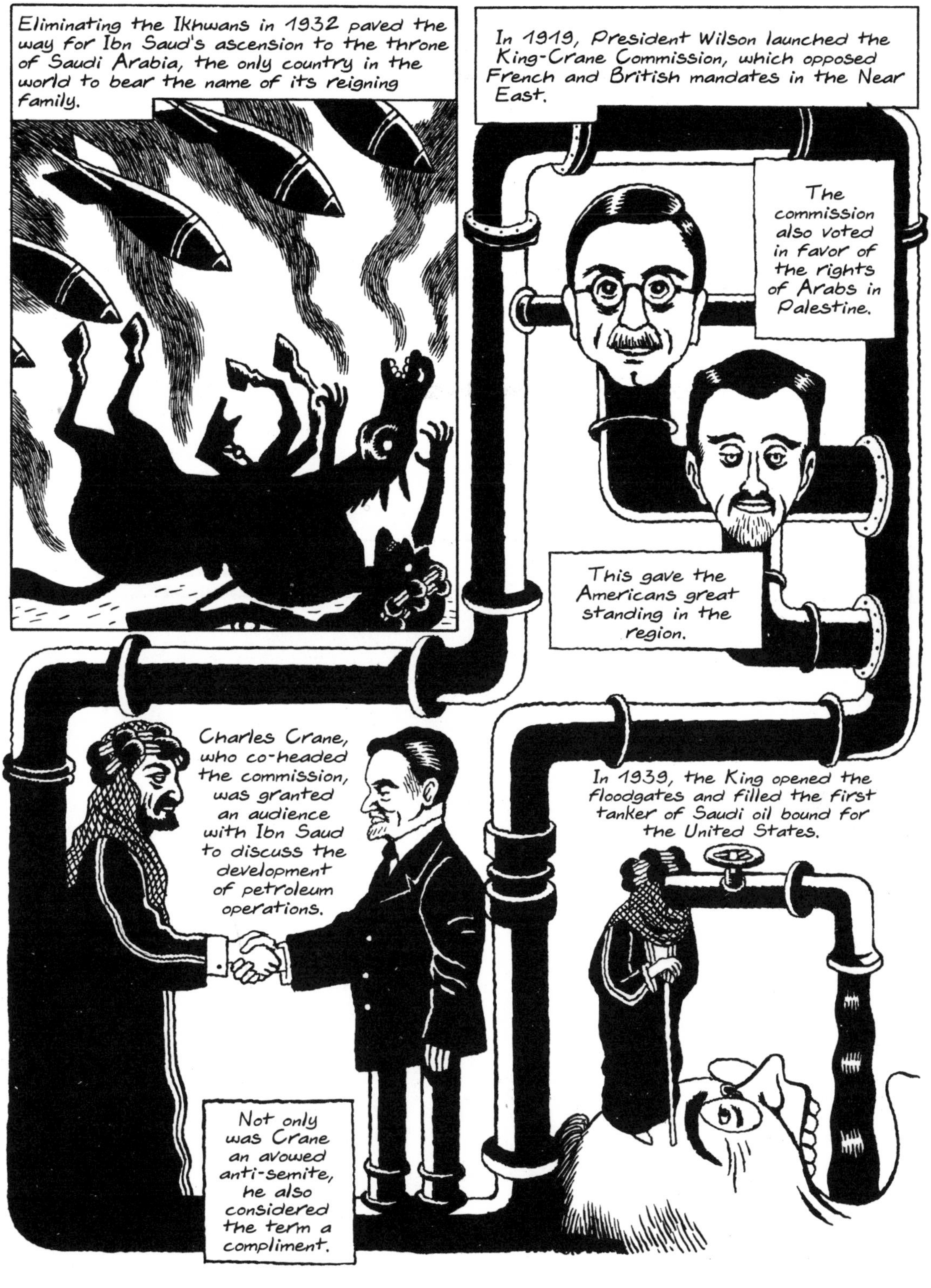

Eliminating the Ikhwans in 1932 paved the way for Ibn Saud's ascension to the throne of Saudi Arabia, the only country in the world to bear the name of its reigning family.
In 1919, President Wilson launched the King-Crane Commission, which opposed French and British mandates in the Near East.
The commission also voted in favor of the rights of Arabs in Palestine.
This gave the Americans great standing in the region.
Charles Crane, who co-headed the commission, was granted an audience with Ibn Saud to discuss the development of petroleum operations.
Not only was Crane an avowed anti-semite, he also considered the term a compliment.
In 1939, the King opened the floodgates and filled the first tanker of Saudi oil bound for the United States.

President Roosevelt made the personal decision to extend Lend-Lease* assistance — originally conceived to aid Britain and the Soviet Union — to Saudi Arabia.

I don't know how we'll convince Congress that Saudi Arabia is a democratic victim of fascist aggression.

Harry Hopkins, adviser to President Roosevelt.

Princes Khaled and Faisal were welcomed in Washington, and plans for a meeting with the King were drawn up.

On 12 February 1945, Ibn Saud and his entourage were received aboard the destroyer USS Murphy, anchored near Djeddah.

* Lend-lease: whereby the US supplied military equipment to the UK and its allies.

On the Saudi side, preparations for the "cruise" took place in utmost secrecy, as it was feared troubles might arise were the King known to have left the country.

Ibn Saud was accompanied by a sizeable entourage — fifty people, not counting sheep.

Believing he would have to feed the *Murphy's* crew, he had brought an entire flock.

The King refused the captain's quarters, and set up camp on the deck.

73

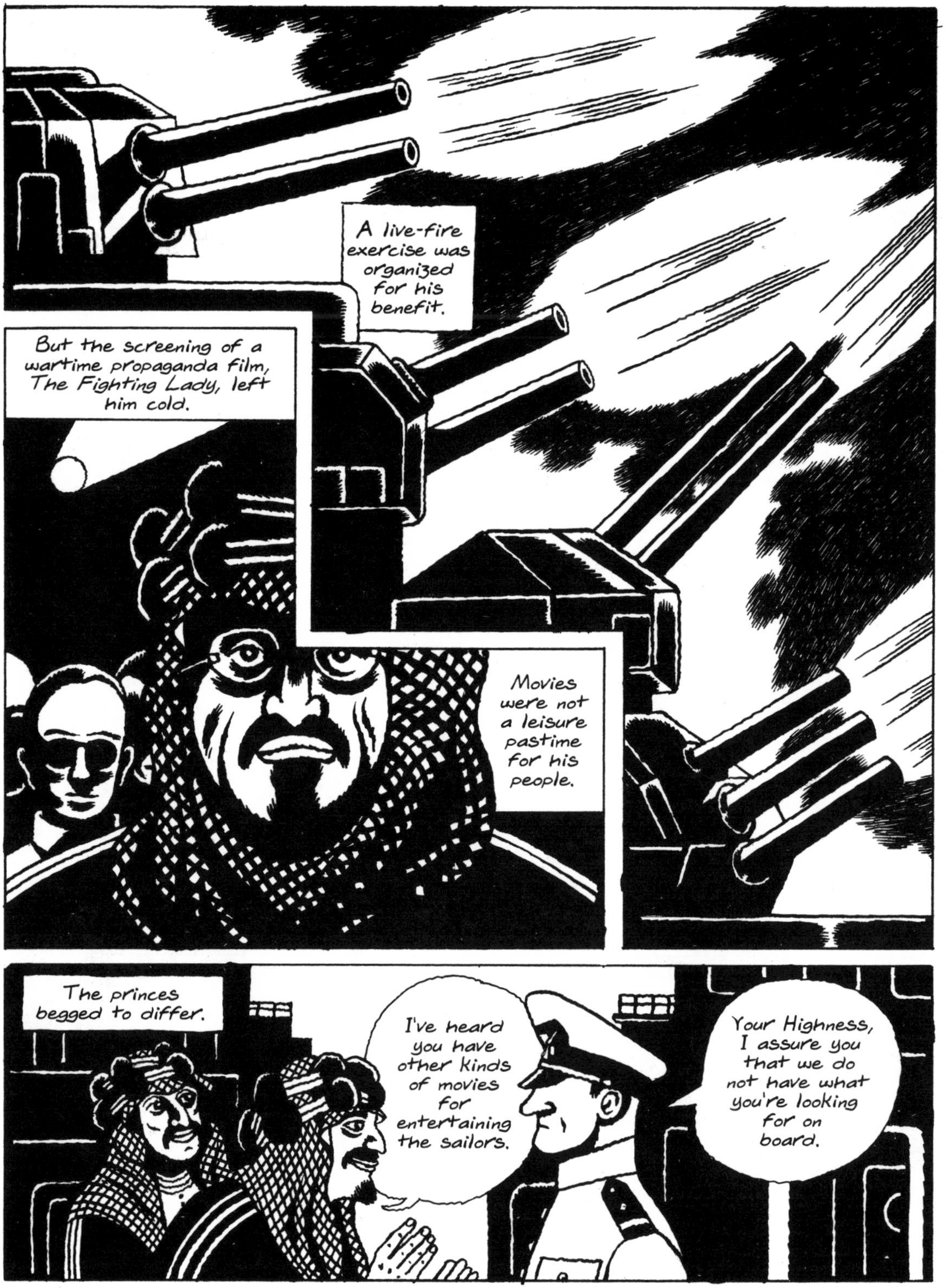
A live-fire exercise was organized for his benefit.
But the screening of a wartime propaganda film, The Fighting Lady, left him cold.
Movies were not a leisure pastime for his people.
The princes begged to differ.
I've heard you have other kinds of movies for entertaining the sailors.
Your Highness, I assure you that we do not have what you're looking for on board.

If you refuse to show us these films, I'll tell my father, and the negotiations will founder!

It is said that, unbeknownst to the King, the princes were treated to scenes somewhat less edifying than those projected that morning.

The King held court in a tent on deck.

He exchanged gifts with the ship's officers.

He kept abreast of the situation abroad by reading news bulletins translated expressly for him.

The summit between the two heads of state took place 14 February 1945 on the USS Quincy.

The American president refrained from drinking.

And though he was a great smoker, forbade cigarettes.

They each had an interpreter: William Eddy for Roosevelt, and Ezzedine Shawa for Ibn Saud.

The two men broke the ice by discussing a shared passion for agricultural work.

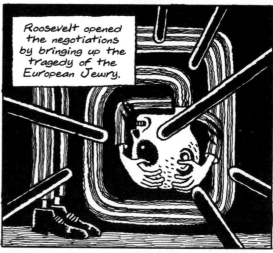
Roosevelt opened the negotiations by bringing up the tragedy of the European Jewry.

For him, it was a moral necessity to grant them free immigration rights to Palestine.

Then give the Jews and their descendants the best land and houses of the Germans who oppressed them.

That is how we settle problems in Arabia, said Ibn Saud: by punishing the guilty person and his family, not by turning against outside parties.

Palestine is a small land, and poor. Its inhabitants have loyally supported the Allied war effort.

Shaken, Roosevelt promised that no decisions would be made regarding Palestine without consulting the Saudis.

He asked Ibn Saud for a formal commitment to the war.

I promise my American friend that we will enter the war on his side.

For Ibn Saud, this "friendship" was a binding pact of tribal solidarity.

The King agreed to the construction of an American base in Dhahran.

A base situated between the war's eastern and western fronts.

The oil agreement was the first to be reached; Saudi royalties rose from eighteen to twenty cents per barrel.

A pipeline would be built to transport oil through Arabia to a port on the eastern Mediterranean.

Both leaders declared themselves satisfied at the end of the meeting.

The U.S. energy supply was assured, in exchange for securing the strategic safety of the Saudi Kingdom.

Once the King was back on land, news of the agreement spread, and the English allies weren't enthusiastic.

Saudi Arabia declared war on the Axis forces in March 1945.

Roosevelt's death a month later did not imperil the agreement...

...even though his successor Harry Truman changed his mind about Palestine, and approved the Zionist project.

The Saudi-American partnership had been founded, and despite crises, endures to this day.

4 Coup d'État

It was the Australian William Knox d'Arcy who, in 1901, began prospecting for oil in Persia.

With support from the United Kingdom, he founded the Anglo-Persian Oil Company (APOC).

In 1914, Winston Churchill acquired a controlling share (51%) in APOC for the British government.

World War I ushered in a definitive change: the Royal Navy switched from coal to petroleum.

To protect their interests in the country during the war, Russian troops occupied the northern part and English troops the oil-rich south.

The two armies had to face local guerrillas.

Persia received royalties of 16% on oil production, and Reza Shah Pahlavi, who succeeded to the throne in 1925, ratified the agreement...

...before denouncing it in 1932 and renegotiating it with the help of the League of Nations. Tehran was guaranteed an annual revenue of one million pounds sterling.

The British concession was extended from 1961 to 1993, and APOC became AIOC.*

* Anglo-Iranian Oil Company

As Reza Shah had pronounced pro-Nazi leanings, Iran found itself occupied once more in 1941: the north by the Soviets and the south by the British.

This double occupation drove Iranians to protest and riot.

The Shah was forced to abdicate in favor of his son Mohammad Reza, who approved of Allied presence in his territory up to six months after the end of the war.

In 1943 Iran declared war on Germany, and the country served as an Allied staging ground.

The Americans embarked on the project of shoring up ports and railroads and, from 1945 onwards, containing Soviet influence in the country.

The Cold War began.

General Herbert Norman Schwarzkopf trained the Iranian army.

The Tudeh, a very powerful Iranian communist party, militated for oil concessions to the USSR, opposing all nationalization in this sector.

In 1943, parliament member Mohammad Mossadegh, launched a campaign in favor of "freedom and independence for Iran".

It demanded the abolition of privileges conceded to London and Moscow.

Americans exerted pressure on Great Britain for the Anglo-Iranian Oil Company to give Iran terms as advantageous as those ARAMCO* had given Saudi Arabia.

* Arabian American Oil Company

London refused, and negotiations stalled.

In March 1951, Prime Minister Ali Razmara was assassinated by a religious extremist.

The Parliament elected Mohammad Mossadegh Prime Minister.

He accepted, on the condition that legislation be put into effect toward the nationalizing of the AIOC.

Fragile of health, he worked from bed.

He received British and American emissaries in his pyjamas...

...and addressed them only in French.

He had studied in France, then made a name for himself in the various posts awarded him.

As a provincial governor and minister, he opposed the stranglehold Britain and the Soviet Union had over his country's economy.

In 1925, he was one of 5 parliament members out of 150 to vote against nominating Reza as the new Shah of Iran.

He was placed under house arrest, and not freed until 1941, when the Allies overthrew the Shah.

Anglophone diplomats did not understand Mossadegh's eccentric way of expressing his nationalism.

The American government increasingly aligned itself with the British "hawks".

American oil companies joined the AIOC's 1951 boycott against Iranian oil. Mossadegh refused to alter his course.

The American Secretary of State spoke of "trench warfare".

Iran lost 40% of its revenue and the crisis grew worse.

Yet in 1952, the Prime Minister was re-elected after three days of violent demonstrations from his supporters.

The International Court of Justice in The Hague came down in favor of Iranian arguments.

For Winston Churchill, overthrowing the government was the only solution. He soon set about implementing it.

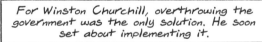

The British Intelligence bet on General Fazlollah Zahedi.

Ambitious, corrupt, and pro-Nazi during World War II, he was the ideal candidate.

But the Prime Minister got wind of the meetings between British agents and the General.

He pulled the rug out from under the conspirators by breaking off diplomatic relations with London in October 1952.

Without diplomatic cover, British spies had to leave the country.

Their Iranian accomplices were left to themselves.

After President Eisenhower's inauguration in January 1953, Washington and London agreed to remove Mossadegh from power.

A first attempt was made on 28 February 1953.

Rioters are coming through the gates!

A crowd of the Shah's supporters, Ayatollah Kashani's loyalists, and henchmen of "Shaban the Brainless" forced their way in.

The Prime Minister barely escaped through the backyard.

He managed to take refuge in Parliament, where he denounced the collusion of the Shah, General Zahedi, and the American Embassy.

In April, Chief of Police Mahmoud Afshartous was kidnapped and killed. This very popular officer might have opposed the coup d'état.

Other targets were considered: generals, ministers, officials. But these murderous gangs were deterred by their bodyguards.

The aim was to plunge the country into chaos.

After two failed attempts, the Eisenhower administration took charge of the process of subversion.

Kermit Roosevelt, the late president's cousin, became operations chief.

He knew the country, and had been head of intelligence there during World War II.

His superiors in the U.S. were the Dulles brothers.

Foster, Secretary of State.

Allen, Director of the CIA.

Kermit Roosevelt got a million dollars to topple Mossadegh.

The coup d'état was to feature several brothers.

In Tehran, Asadollah, Qodratollah, and Seyfollah Rashidian were influential agents in the plot.

They stirred up their networks, not only in politics, but in the press and on the street.

The CIA codenamed two riot organizers, Ali Jalili and Farouk Keyvani, as "the brothers".

General Zahedi spearheaded the plot, relying on officers of all stripes.

Ayatollah Kashani joined the conspirators, providing religious support.

The young Mullah Khomeini denounced the Mossadegh government.

And then there were those who made up the mobs.

All the little hands and fists that go into an uprising.

And then there was the Shah.

Nothing could happen without him, but he didn't dare commit himself.

I'm afraid...

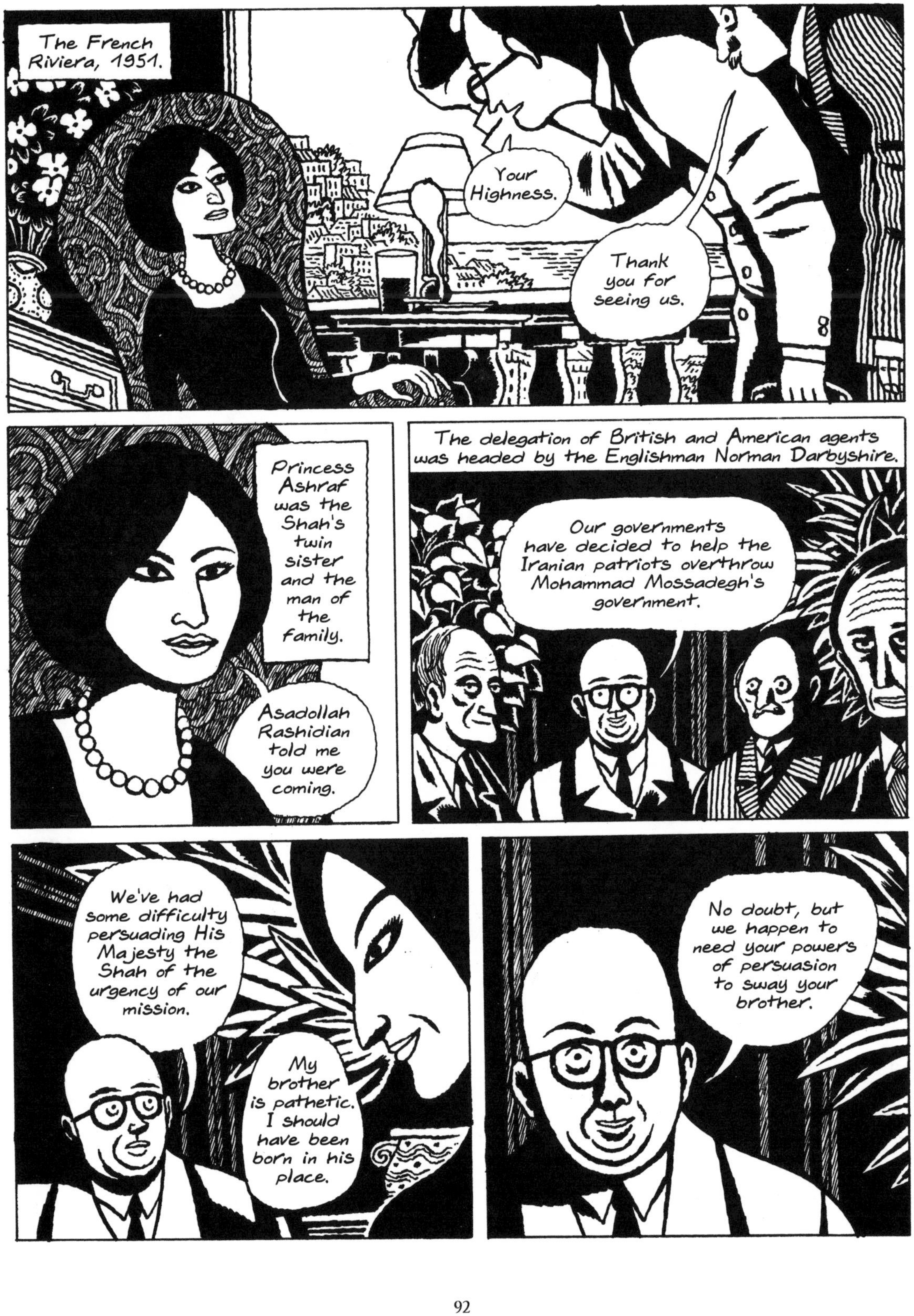
The French Riviera, 1951.
Your Highness.
Thank you for seeing us.
Princess Ashraf was the Shah's twin sister and the man of the family.
Asadollah Rashidian told me you were coming.
The delegation of British and American agents was headed by the Englishman Norman Darbyshire.
Our governments have decided to help the Iranian patriots overthrow Mohammad Mossadegh's government.
We've had some difficulty persuading His Majesty the Shah of the urgency of our mission.
My brother is pathetic. I should have been born in his place.
No doubt, but we happen to need your powers of persuasion to sway your brother.

That would be utterly useless. As I've already said, he is, quite simply, a weakling.

We're agreed there.

But it won't cost you a thing to make this overture.

We've brought you something to cover your expenses.

I'll do everything I can.

We thought you might like this coat.

I'll leave for Tehran tomorrow.

At first, the Shah refused to see his sister.

But he had to.

Princess Ashraf did not manage to persuade him.

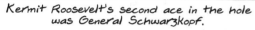

Kermit Roosevelt's second ace in the hole was General Schwarzkopf.

In the last war, he had trained a unit of the Iranian army.

Things were quite well arranged. The general suddenly needed to make a tour of inspection from Egypt to Pakistan, and had to stop over in Iran.

Hello, Kermit!

General, we've a lot of work to do.

He did not come empty-handed, distributing money to America's Iranian agents.

He obtained an audience with the Shah, who was behaving strangely...

Your Majesty.

?

The silent Shah dragged him into the maze of the palace's empty halls.

I was afraid it might be bugged. Sit down beside me.

Mr. Kermit Roosevelt asked me to sign an edict dismissing Mossadegh. I'm not sure I can.

I'm afraid the army will refuse to obey my orders. Two attempts have failed already. I can't risk ending up on the wrong side.

Your Majesty...

Do you want to risk seeing your country sink into communism like Korea? There's no other way.

I'll ask Kermit Roosevelt to come see you at the palace. He'll settle all the details.

No! No, no I don't want him seen here!

We'll take care of everything.

Kermit Roosevelt sought a secret meeting with the Shah, implying that he had no choice.

Late that night, a car came to pick up Kermit Roosevelt.

He was taken to a hidden entrance in the gardens of the palace.

Good evening, Mr. Roosevelt.

Evening, Your Majesty.

I came to your country on behalf of American and British intelligence.

A code phrase tomorrow night at the end of BBC programming will confirm this.

I need to be sure that Churchill's on my side. I'm not one for adventures.

You're the ruler and that's why you alone can sign an edict discharging Prime Minister Mossadegh.

If he stays in power, your country will fall into communist hands, and our governments aren't prepared to let that happen.

His expulsion will only reinforce his power.

If you refuse to help us, we'll find other solutions.

Let's meet again tomorrow night to discuss details, Mr. Roosevelt.

And that's the end of our programming here on the BBC. It's almost midnight...

"Almost midnight."

The code phrase.

There we are.

Kermit Roosevelt and the Shah met again over the next few nights.

Bit by bit, the American agent managed to convince the sovereign.

I agree to sign the edicts discharging him.

But during the coup, I'll be at my hunting lodge in Ramsar. I don't want to stay in Tehran.

The Shah left for Ramsar, "forgetting" to sign the edicts.

His chief bodyguard came in person to make him sign them.

At last.

The edicts were carefully kept at the American Embassy in case the Shah changed his mind.

CIA agents celebrated their victory with a terrific bender.

Operation Ajax, named after the Greek hero from the Iliad, had begun.

It got off to a bad start.

Colonel Nasiri was in charge of arresting Mossadegh at home.

Arrest the Prime Minister?

No, Colonel, it is you who are under arrest!

But Kermit Roosevelt did not back down, and intensified his anti-government propaganda.

Bribed reporters launched highly vicious campaigns.

The Shah's favorites were threatened by unnamed people claiming to be Mossadegh's supporters.

Mullahs who'd been bought off denounced Mossadegh in their sermons.

Tracts defaming the collusion between the Prime Minister and communists were handed out in the street.

Corrupt politicians attacked him in Parliament.

False protesters, paid a daily wage, began appearing in public.

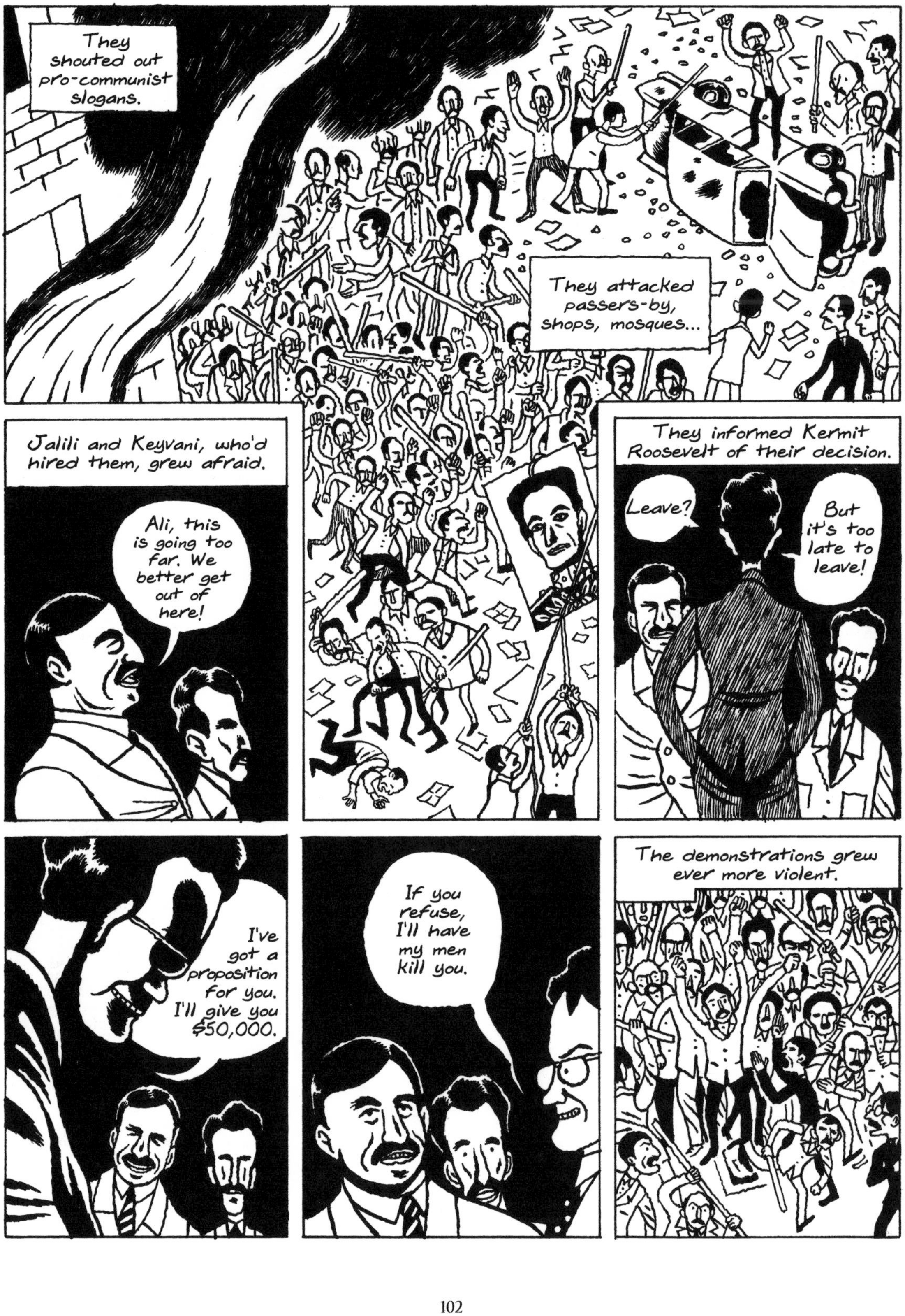
They shouted out pro-communist slogans.
They attacked passers-by, shops, mosques...
Jalili and Keyvani, who'd hired them, grew afraid.
Ali, this is going too far. We better get out of here!
They informed Kermit Roosevelt of their decision.
Leave?
But it's too late to leave!
I've got a proposition for you. I'll give you $50,000.
If you refuse, I'll have my men kill you.
The demonstrations grew ever more violent.

The Shah distanced himself from events.

He fled first to Iraq, then to Rome.

General Zahedi and other high-ranking officers took shelter in the American Embassy.

Rumor spread through the largely loyalist Army that the officers arrested with Colonel Nasiri were to be shot.

In the street, the false protesters had attracted real ones who thought the hour of revolution had come, and took part in the looting.

Other activists, sensing the trap, tried to stop the violence.

It was chaos.

Stalin had died shortly before, and in the Soviet Union, the race to succeed him was on.

As a result, the Iranian Communist Party received no guidance.

Increasingly, the mob struck out at images of the Shah with slogans and violent acts...

...which had the effect of toppling several police and army officers in the anti-government camp.

Just as Mossadegh had refused to silence the newspapers slandering him...

...so he refused to put a halt to the demonstrations.

Which delighted Kermit Roosevelt.

But Mossadegh couldn't afford to let the situation degenerate. He ordered the police to clear the streets.

Which only served to delight Roosevelt further.

General Daftary was charged with crowd control.

A task he carried out with all the more zeal as he was on the side of the coup.

Mossadegh ended up banning all demonstrations.

He called his closest supporters and asked them not to go into the streets.

For the streets belonged to the army and the police.

Kermit Roosevelt organized processions on the Shah's behalf.

These were entirely peaceful.

All the more so, since they were flanked by the army and the police...

...and guided by very popular "pahlavans", members of wrestling clubs linked to the underworld.

From outside the city arrived groups of nomadic tribesmen.

The CIA had paid their chieftains to mobilize them.

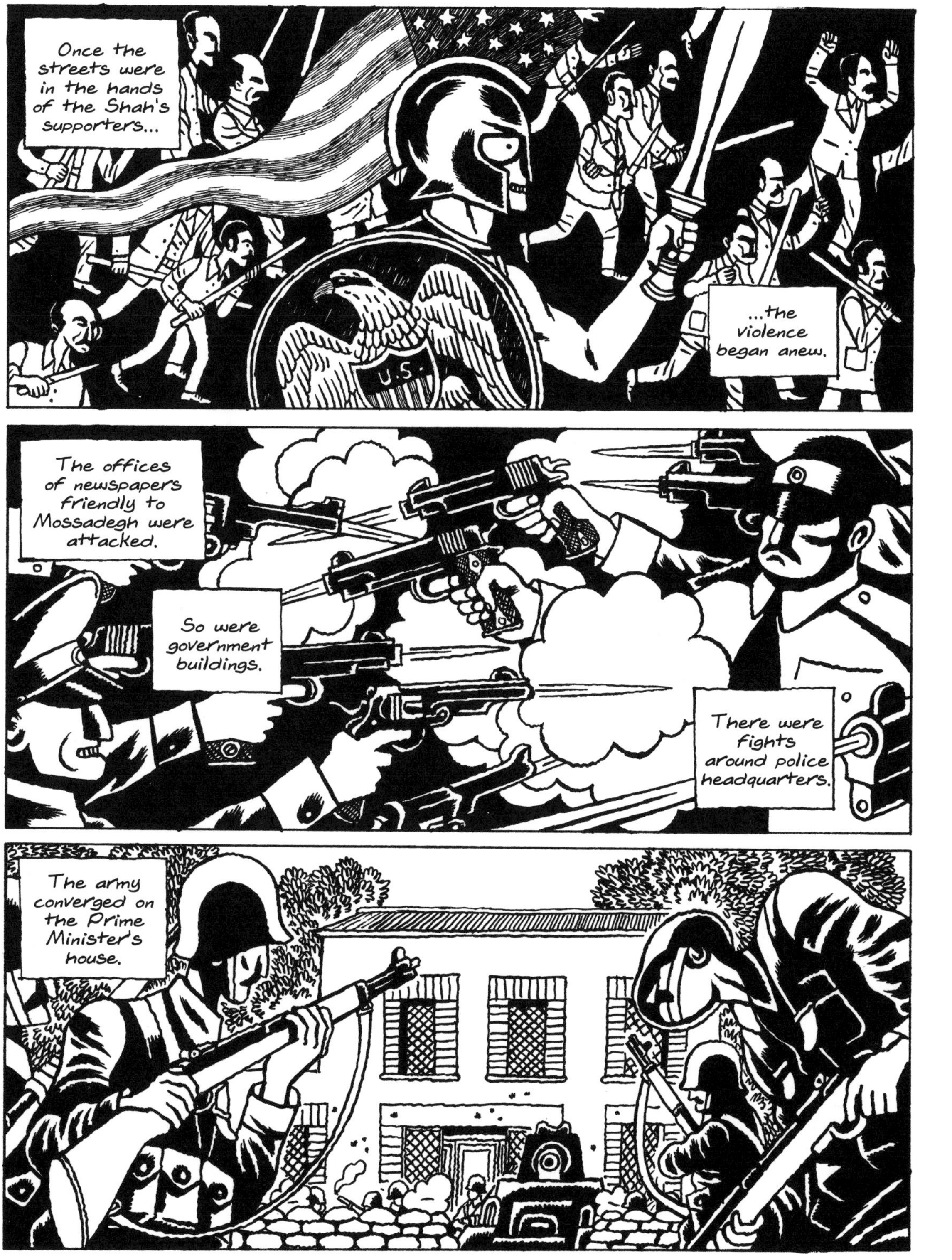
Once the streets were in the hands of the Shah's supporters...
...the violence began anew.
U.S.
The offices of newspapers friendly to Mossadegh were attacked.
So were government buildings.
There were fights around police headquarters.
The army converged on the Prime Minister's house.

At the American Embassy, Kermit Roosevelt found General Zahedi in his underwear.

Why, General! Get dressed!

Is it really happening?

Two tanks were waiting to escort him to the radio station.

Find suitably formal music to introduce my speech.

By accident, the technician started playing the first few bars of the American national anthem.

After a few anxious moments, General Zahedi began his address.

By order of his Majesty the Shah —

Mohammad Mossadegh is dismissed, and I will assume the office of Prime Minister.

In Rome, reporters informed the Shah that the Prime Minister had been overthrown.

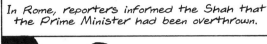

At first, the Shah was incredulous.

Can it be?

Can it really be?

I knew it!

My people love me.

In Tehran, Mossadegh's house was the site of the loyalist troops' last stand against the coup.

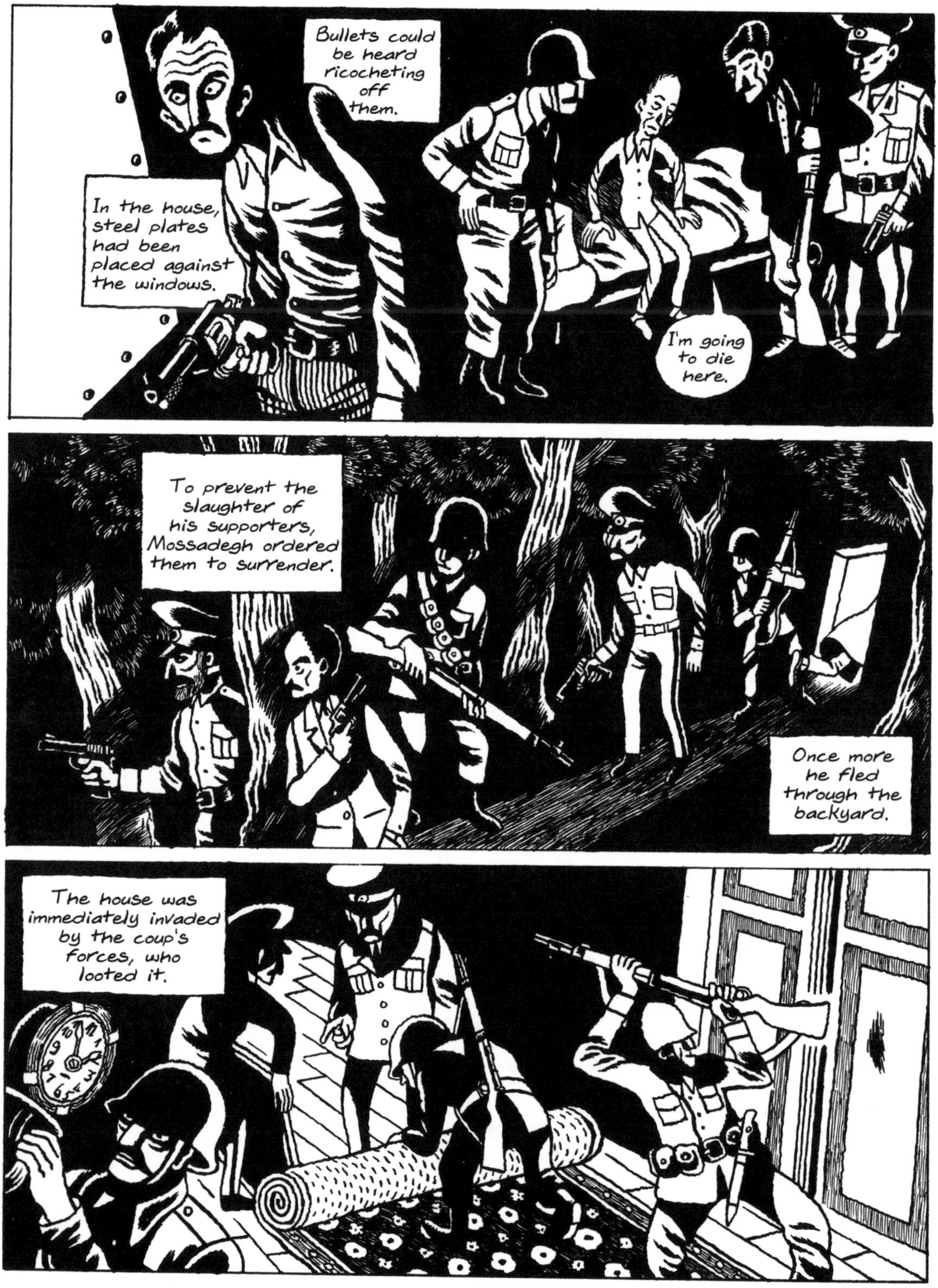
In the house, steel plates had been placed against the windows.
Bullets could be heard ricocheting off them.
I'm going to die here.
To prevent the slaughter of his supporters, Mossadegh ordered them to surrender.
Once more he fled through the backyard.
The house was immediately invaded by the coup's forces, who looted it.

Furniture and belongings were loaded onto trucks and hauled off.

After the troops came the mob of rioters, who finished sacking the house before burning it to the ground.

Bodies of the dead were gathered. 500-rial bills were found in the pockets of civilians — their pay for participating in the protests.

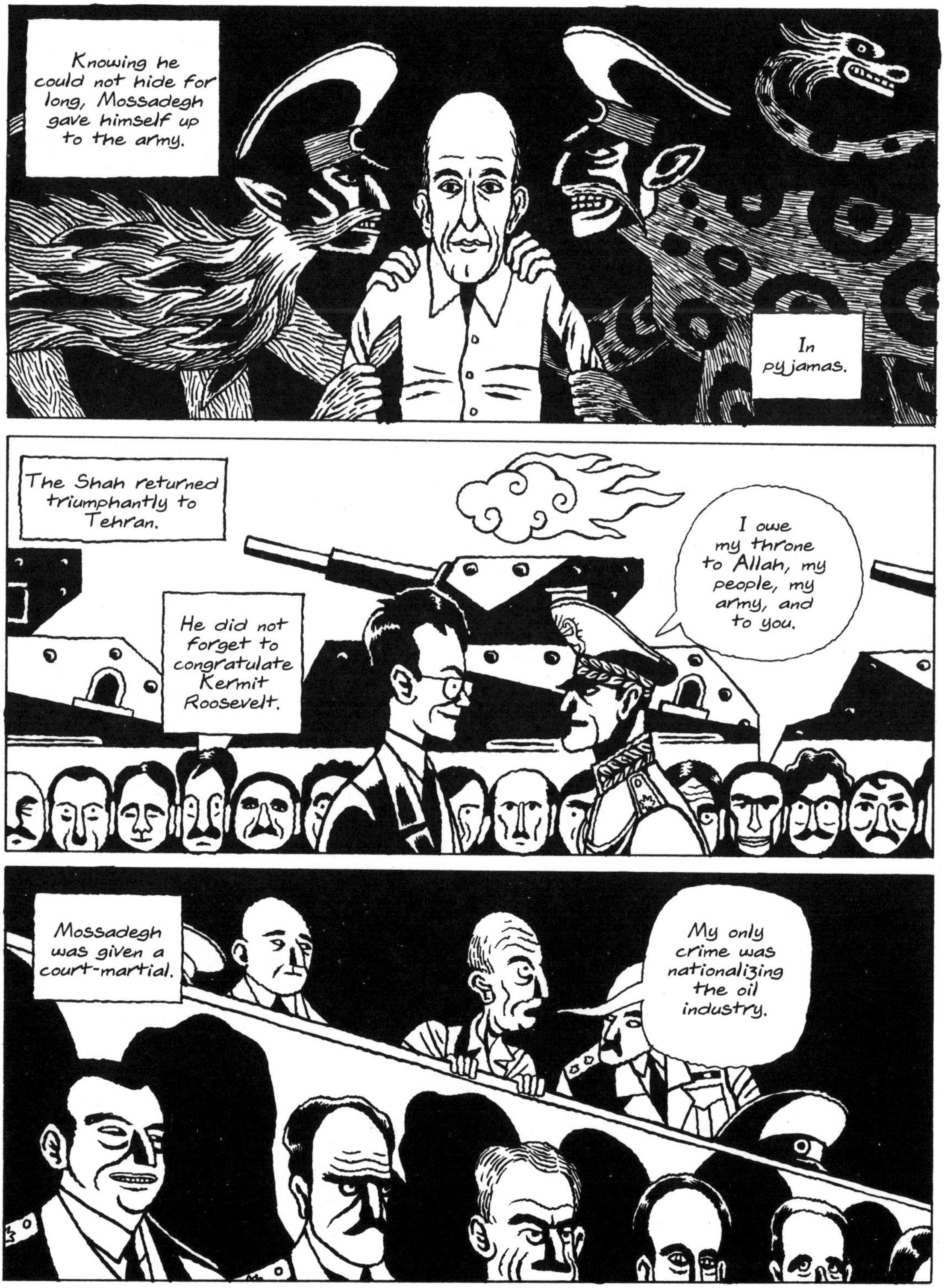
Knowing he could not hide for long, Mossadegh gave himself up to the army.
In pyjamas.
The Shah returned triumphantly to Tehran.
He did not forget to congratulate Kermit Roosevelt.
I owe my throne to Allah, my people, my army, and to you.
Mossadegh was given a court-martial.
My only crime was nationalizing the oil industry.

The trial gave rise to one last heated exchange between the Shah and his former Prime Minster.

I defy anyone to prove that his overthrow was not the work of the ordinary people of my country, in whose hearts is the spark of the divine.

The divine spark in Eisenhower's heart led to selling off our nation's freedom cheaply for a 40% share in the oil consortium.

Mossadegh was sentenced to three years in prison.

He refused the Shah's pardon.

He was freed in 1956, and spent the rest of his life under house arrest.

He spent his time reading and cooking. One of his favorite books was an encylopedia of cooking.

He died in 1967.

For the CIA, Operation Ajax was a success: limited costs with considerable impact.

It served as a model for the 1954 coup that toppled President Árbenz Guzmán in Guatemala.

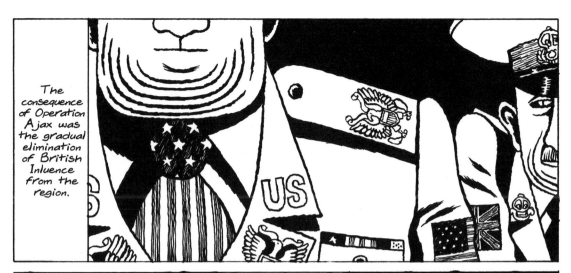

The consequence of Operation Ajax was the gradual elimination of British Inluence from the region.

This found expression in President Eisenhower's 1956 opposition to the coordinated French, British, and Israeli offensive against Egypt.

The era of the colonial powers was over. The American era had begun.

About the Author

Jean-Pierre Filiu, a historian and an arabist, is professor at Sciences Po, Paris School of International Affairs (PSIA). After an extensive career in the Middle East, first with NGOs, then as a diplomat, he has held visiting professorships both at Columbia (New York) and at Georgetown (Washington). His *Apocalypse in Islam* (University of California Press, 2011) was awarded the main prize by the French History Convention. His works and articles about contemporary Islam have been published in a dozen languages. His most recent book is *Arab Revolution: Ten Lessons from the Democratic Uprising* (Hurst, London and Oxford University Press, New York).

About the Author/Artist

David B. is the Eisner Award-nominated artist behind *Epileptic*, an autobiographical story widely considered a masterpiece of the graphic-novel medium. A founding member of the revolutionary French independent publisher L'Association, he is regarded as a giant among Bandes Dessinées artists. His many prizes include the Prix de Cheverny (2007), the Ignatz Award for Outstanding Artist (2005), and the top prizes for Comics Writing (2002) and Best Comic Book (1998, 2004) at the Angoulême International Comics Festival. His *Black Paths* – the extraordinary story of the Dadaist poet Gabriele d'Annunzio – was published by SelfMadeHero in 2011.